NAME:

HIKING LOGBOOK

"**Travel** makes one modest.
You see what a tiny place
you occupy in the **World**."
–Gustave Flaubert

HIKING LOGBOOK

DATE: ☀ ⛅ ☁ 🌧 ⛈ ❄ 🌫 💨 ☐ Hot ☐ Cold ☐ Mild

Start Time: _____ End Time: _____

Total Duration: _____ Total Distance: _____

Elevation Gain/Loss: _____

Trail Type (circle one): Out & Back Loop One Way / Shuttle

THE HIKE ☆ ☆ ☆ ☆ ☆

City/State: _____

Trail(s): _____

Start Latitude/Longitude: _____

Terrain: _____

Cell Phone Reception/Carrier: _____

☐ First Visit ☐ Return Visit Personal Rating: Easy / Intermediate / Difficult

Companion(s): _____

Facilities / Water Availability?: _____

Trail & Weather Conditions: _____

Observances (wildlife, nature, views, etc): _____

Gear, Food & Beverages: _____

Notes for next time (shuttles, entrance fees, parking, routes, pets, etc): _____

NOTES / JOURNALING

HIKING LOGBOOK

DATE: ☼ ⛅ ☁ ☂ ⛈ ❄ 🌫 ☐Hot ☐Cold ☐Mild

Start Time:_____ End Time:_____

Total Duration:_____ Total Distance:_____

Elevation Gain/Loss:_____

Trail Type (circle one):　　Out & Back　　Loop　　One Way / Shuttle

THE HIKE　　☆ ☆ ☆ ☆ ☆

City/State:_____

Trail(s):_____

_____

Start Latitude/Longitude:_____

Terrain:_____

Cell Phone Reception/Carrier:_____

☐First Visit　☐Return Visit　　Personal Rating: Easy / Intermediate / Difficult

Companion(s):_____

Facilities / Water Availability?:_____

Trail & Weather Conditions:_____

Observances (wildlife, nature, views, etc):_____

Gear, Food & Beverages:_____

Notes for next time (shuttles, entrance fees, parking, routes, pets, etc):_____

_____

NOTES / JOURNALING

HIKING LOGBOOK

DATE: ☼ ⛅ ☁ 🌧 ⛈ ❄ 🌫 ☐Hot ☐Cold ☐Mild

Start Time:_____ End Time:_____

Total Duration:_____ Total Distance:_____

Elevation Gain/Loss:_____

Trail Type (circle one):   Out & Back   Loop   One Way / Shuttle

THE HIKE   ☆ ☆ ☆ ☆ ☆

City/State:_____

Trail(s):_____
_____

Start Latitude/Longitude:_____

Terrain:_____

Cell Phone Reception/Carrier:_____

☐First Visit   ☐Return Visit   Personal Rating: Easy / Intermediate / Difficult

Companion(s):_____

Facilities / Water Availability?:_____

Trail & Weather Conditions:_____

Observances (wildlife, nature, views, etc):_____

Gear, Food & Beverages:_____

Notes for next time (shuttles, entrance fees, parking, routes, pets, etc):_____
_____

NOTES / JOURNALING

HIKING LOGBOOK

DATE: ☀ ⛅ ☁ ☁ 🌧 ❄ 🌬 ☐Hot ☐Cold ☐Mild

Start Time:_____ End Time:_____

Total Duration:_____ Total Distance:_____

Elevation Gain/Loss:_____

Trail Type (circle one):   Out & Back   Loop   One Way / Shuttle

THE HIKE   ☆ ☆ ☆ ☆ ☆

City/State:_____

Trail(s):_____

Start Latitude/Longitude:_____

Terrain:_____

Cell Phone Reception/Carrier:_____

☐First Visit   ☐Return Visit   Personal Rating: Easy / Intermediate / Difficult

Companion(s):_____

Facilities / Water Availability?:_____

Trail & Weather Conditions:_____

Observances (wildlife, nature, views, etc):_____

Gear, Food & Beverages:_____

Notes for next time (shuttles, entrance fees, parking, routes, pets, etc):_____

NOTES / JOURNALING

HIKING LOGBOOK

DATE: ☀ ⛅ ☁ 🌧 ⛈ ❄ 🌫 ☐Hot ☐Cold ☐Mild

Start Time:_____ End Time:_____

Total Duration:_____ Total Distance:_____

Elevation Gain/Loss:_____

Trail Type (circle one):   Out & Back   Loop   One Way / Shuttle

THE HIKE ☆☆☆☆☆

City/State:_____

Trail(s):_____
_____

Start Latitude/Longitude:_____

Terrain:_____

Cell Phone Reception/Carrier:_____

☐First Visit ☐Return Visit   Personal Rating: Easy / Intermediate / Difficult

Companion(s):_____

Facilities / Water Availability?:_____

Trail & Weather Conditions:_____

Observances (wildlife, nature, views, etc):_____

Gear, Food & Beverages:_____

Notes for next time (shuttles, entrance fees, parking, routes, pets, etc):_____
_____

NOTES / JOURNALING

HIKING LOGBOOK

DATE: ☼ ⛅ ☁ 🌧 ⛈ ❄ 🌫 ☐Hot ☐Cold ☐Mild

Start Time: _____ End Time: _____

Total Duration: _____ Total Distance: _____

Elevation Gain/Loss: _____

Trail Type (circle one): Out & Back Loop One Way / Shuttle

THE HIKE ☆ ☆ ☆ ☆ ☆

City/State: _____

Trail(s): _____

Start Latitude/Longitude: _____

Terrain: _____

Cell Phone Reception/Carrier: _____

☐First Visit ☐Return Visit Personal Rating: Easy / Intermediate / Difficult

Companion(s): _____

Facilities / Water Availability?: _____

Trail & Weather Conditions: _____

Observances (wildlife, nature, views, etc): _____

Gear, Food & Beverages: _____

Notes for next time (shuttles, entrance fees, parking, routes, pets, etc): _____

Notes / Journaling

HIKING LOGBOOK

DATE: ☀ ⛅ ☁ ☁ 🌧 ⛈ ❄ 🌬 ☐Hot ☐Cold ☐Mild

Start Time: _____   End Time: _____

Total Duration: _____   Total Distance: _____

Elevation Gain/Loss: _____

Trail Type (circle one):   Out & Back   Loop   One Way / Shuttle

THE HIKE   ☆ ☆ ☆ ☆ ☆

City/State: _____

Trail(s): _____

Start Latitude/Longitude: _____

Terrain: _____

Cell Phone Reception/Carrier: _____

☐First Visit   ☐Return Visit   Personal Rating: Easy / Intermediate / Difficult

Companion(s): _____

Facilities / Water Availability?: _____

Trail & Weather Conditions: _____

Observances (wildlife, nature, views, etc): _____

Gear, Food & Beverages: _____

Notes for next time (shuttles, entrance fees, parking, routes, pets, etc): _____

NOTES / JOURNALING

HIKING LOGBOOK

DATE: ☀ ⛅ ☁ 🌧 ⛈ ❄ 🌫 ☐Hot ☐Cold ☐Mild

Start Time: _____   End Time: _____

Total Duration: _____   Total Distance: _____

Elevation Gain/Loss: _____

Trail Type (circle one):   Out & Back   Loop   One Way / Shuttle

THE HIKE   ☆ ☆ ☆ ☆ ☆

City/State: _____

Trail(s): _____

Start Latitude/Longitude: _____

Terrain: _____

Cell Phone Reception/Carrier: _____

☐First Visit   ☐Return Visit   Personal Rating: Easy / Intermediate / Difficult

Companion(s): _____

Facilities / Water Availability?: _____

Trail & Weather Conditions: _____

Observances (wildlife, nature, views, etc): _____

Gear, Food & Beverages: _____

Notes for next time (shuttles, entrance fees, parking, routes, pets, etc): _____

NOTES / JOURNALING

HIKING LOGBOOK

DATE: ☼ ⛅ ☁ 🌧 ⛈ ❄ 🌫 ☐Hot ☐Cold ☐Mild

Start Time: _____   End Time: _____

Total Duration: _____   Total Distance: _____

Elevation Gain/Loss: _____

Trail Type (circle one):   Out & Back   Loop   One Way / Shuttle

THE HIKE   ☆ ☆ ☆ ☆ ☆

City/State: _____

Trail(s): _____

Start Latitude/Longitude: _____

Terrain: _____

Cell Phone Reception/Carrier: _____

☐First Visit ☐Return Visit   Personal Rating: Easy / Intermediate / Difficult

Companion(s): _____

Facilities / Water Availability?: _____

Trail & Weather Conditions: _____

Observances (wildlife, nature, views, etc): _____

Gear, Food & Beverages: _____

Notes for next time (shuttles, entrance fees, parking, routes, pets, etc): _____

NOTES / JOURNALING

HIKING LOGBOOK

DATE: ☀ ⛅ ☁ ☁ 🌧 🌩 ❄ 🌬 ☐Hot ☐Cold ☐Mild

Start Time:_____   End Time:_____

Total Duration:_____   Total Distance:_____

Elevation Gain/Loss:_____

Trail Type (circle one):   Out & Back   Loop   One Way / Shuttle

THE HIKE   ☆ ☆ ☆ ☆ ☆

City/State:_____

Trail(s):_____

Start Latitude/Longitude:_____

Terrain:_____

Cell Phone Reception/Carrier:_____

☐First Visit   ☐Return Visit   Personal Rating: Easy / Intermediate / Difficult

Companion(s):_____

Facilities / Water Availability?:_____

Trail & Weather Conditions:_____

Observances (wildlife, nature, views, etc):_____

Gear, Food & Beverages:_____

Notes for next time (shuttles, entrance fees, parking, routes, pets, etc):_____

NOTES / JOURNALING

HIKING LOGBOOK

DATE: ☀ ⛅ ☁ ☂ ⛈ ❄ 🌫 ☐Hot ☐Cold ☐Mild

Start Time:_____ End Time:_____

Total Duration:_____ Total Distance:_____

Elevation Gain/Loss:_____

Trail Type (circle one):　　Out & Back　　Loop　　One Way / Shuttle

THE HIKE ☆☆☆☆☆

City/State:_____

Trail(s):_____

Start Latitude/Longitude:_____

Terrain:_____

Cell Phone Reception/Carrier:_____

☐First Visit　☐Return Visit　　Personal Rating: Easy / Intermediate / Difficult

Companion(s):_____

Facilities / Water Availability?:_____

Trail & Weather Conditions:_____

Observances (wildlife, nature, views, etc):_____

Gear, Food & Beverages:_____

Notes for next time (shuttles, entrance fees, parking, routes, pets, etc):_____

NOTES / JOURNALING

HIKING LOGBOOK

DATE: ☼ ⛅ ☁ 🌧 ⛈ ❄ 🌫 ☐Hot ☐Cold ☐Mild

Start Time:_____ End Time:_____

Total Duration:_____ Total Distance:_____

Elevation Gain/Loss:_____

Trail Type (circle one):   Out & Back   Loop   One Way / Shuttle

THE HIKE   ☆ ☆ ☆ ☆ ☆

City/State:_____

Trail(s):_____

Start Latitude/Longitude:_____

Terrain:_____

Cell Phone Reception/Carrier:_____

☐First Visit   ☐Return Visit   Personal Rating: Easy / Intermediate / Difficult

Companion(s):_____

Facilities / Water Availability?:_____

Trail & Weather Conditions:_____

Observances (wildlife, nature, views, etc):_____

Gear, Food & Beverages:_____

Notes for next time (shuttles, entrance fees, parking, routes, pets, etc):_____

NOTES / JOURNALING

HIKING LOGBOOK

DATE: ☐Hot ☐Cold ☐Mild

Start Time:_____ End Time:_____

Total Duration:_____ Total Distance:_____

Elevation Gain/Loss:_____

Trail Type (circle one):   Out & Back   Loop   One Way / Shuttle

THE HIKE ☆☆☆☆☆

City/State:_____

Trail(s):_____

Start Latitude/Longitude:_____

Terrain:_____

Cell Phone Reception/Carrier:_____

☐First Visit ☐Return Visit   Personal Rating: Easy / Intermediate / Difficult

Companion(s):_____

Facilities / Water Availability?:_____

Trail & Weather Conditions:_____

Observances (wildlife, nature, views, etc):_____

Gear, Food & Beverages:_____

Notes for next time (shuttles, entrance fees, parking, routes, pets, etc):_____

NOTES / JOURNALING

HIKING LOGBOOK

DATE: ☀ ⛅ ☁ 🌧 ⛈ ❄ 🌫 ☐Hot ☐Cold ☐Mild

Start Time:_____ End Time:_____

Total Duration:_____ Total Distance:_____

Elevation Gain/Loss:_____

Trail Type (circle one):   Out & Back   Loop   One Way / Shuttle

THE HIKE   ☆ ☆ ☆ ☆ ☆

City/State:_____

Trail(s):_____

Start Latitude/Longitude:_____

Terrain:_____

Cell Phone Reception/Carrier:_____

☐First Visit   ☐Return Visit   Personal Rating: Easy / Intermediate / Difficult

Companion(s):_____

Facilities / Water Availability?:_____

Trail & Weather Conditions:_____

Observances (wildlife, nature, views, etc):_____

Gear, Food & Beverages:_____

Notes for next time (shuttles, entrance fees, parking, routes, pets, etc):_____

NOTES / JOURNALING

HIKING LOGBOOK

DATE: ☼ ⛅ ☁ ☁ 🌦 ⛈ ❄ 🌫 ☐Hot ☐Cold ☐Mild

Start Time: _____ End Time: _____

Total Duration: _____ Total Distance: _____

Elevation Gain/Loss: _____

Trail Type (circle one):   Out & Back   Loop   One Way / Shuttle

THE HIKE ☆☆☆☆☆

City/State: _____

Trail(s): _____

Start Latitude/Longitude: _____

Terrain: _____

Cell Phone Reception/Carrier: _____

☐First Visit   ☐Return Visit   Personal Rating: Easy / Intermediate / Difficult

Companion(s): _____

Facilities / Water Availability?: _____

Trail & Weather Conditions: _____

Observances (wildlife, nature, views, etc): _____

Gear, Food & Beverages: _____

Notes for next time (shuttles, entrance fees, parking, routes, pets, etc): _____

NOTES / JOURNALING

HIKING LOGBOOK

DATE: ☀ ⛅ ⛅ ☁ 🌧 ⛈ ❄ 🌬 ☐Hot ☐Cold ☐Mild

Start Time:_____ End Time:_____

Total Duration:_____ Total Distance:_____

Elevation Gain/Loss:_____

Trail Type (circle one):   Out & Back   Loop   One Way / Shuttle

THE HIKE   ☆ ☆ ☆ ☆ ☆

City/State:_____

Trail(s):_____

Start Latitude/Longitude:_____

Terrain:_____

Cell Phone Reception/Carrier:_____

☐First Visit   ☐Return Visit   Personal Rating: Easy / Intermediate / Difficult

Companion(s):_____

Facilities / Water Availability?:_____

Trail & Weather Conditions:_____

Observances (wildlife, nature, views, etc):_____

Gear, Food & Beverages:_____

Notes for next time (shuttles, entrance fees, parking, routes, pets, etc):_____

NOTES / JOURNALING

HIKING LOGBOOK

DATE: ☀ ⛅ ☁ 🌧 ⛈ ❄ 🌫 ☐Hot ☐Cold ☐Mild

Start Time:_____   End Time:_____

Total Duration:_____   Total Distance:_____

Elevation Gain/Loss:_____

Trail Type (circle one):   Out & Back   Loop   One Way / Shuttle

THE HIKE   ☆ ☆ ☆ ☆ ☆

City/State:_____

Trail(s):_____

Start Latitude/Longitude:_____

Terrain:_____

Cell Phone Reception/Carrier:_____

☐First Visit   ☐Return Visit   Personal Rating: Easy / Intermediate / Difficult

Companion(s):_____

Facilities / Water Availability?:_____

Trail & Weather Conditions:_____

Observances (wildlife, nature, views, etc):_____

Gear, Food & Beverages:_____

Notes for next time (shuttles, entrance fees, parking, routes, pets, etc):_____

NOTES / JOURNALING

HIKING LOGBOOK

DATE: ☀ ⛅ ☁ 🌧 ⛈ ❄ 🌫 ☐Hot ☐Cold ☐Mild

Start Time:_____ End Time:_____

Total Duration:_____ Total Distance:_____

Elevation Gain/Loss:_____

Trail Type (circle one): Out & Back   Loop   One Way / Shuttle

THE HIKE ☆☆☆☆☆

City/State:_____

Trail(s):_____

Start Latitude/Longitude:_____

Terrain:_____

Cell Phone Reception/Carrier:_____

☐First Visit ☐Return Visit   Personal Rating: Easy / Intermediate / Difficult

Companion(s):_____

Facilities / Water Availability?:_____

Trail & Weather Conditions:_____

Observances (wildlife, nature, views, etc):_____

Gear, Food & Beverages:_____

Notes for next time (shuttles, entrance fees, parking, routes, pets, etc):_____

NOTES / JOURNALING

HIKING LOGBOOK

DATE: ☼ ⛅ ☁ ☁ 🌧 ⛈ ❄ 🌫 ☐Hot ☐Cold ☐Mild

Start Time:_____ End Time:_____

Total Duration:_____ Total Distance:_____

Elevation Gain/Loss:_____

Trail Type (circle one):   Out & Back   Loop   One Way / Shuttle

THE HIKE   ☆ ☆ ☆ ☆ ☆

City/State:_____

Trail(s):_____

Start Latitude/Longitude:_____

Terrain:_____

Cell Phone Reception/Carrier:_____

☐First Visit   ☐Return Visit   Personal Rating: Easy / Intermediate / Difficult

Companion(s):_____

Facilities / Water Availability?:_____

Trail & Weather Conditions:_____

Observances (wildlife, nature, views, etc):_____

Gear, Food & Beverages:_____

Notes for next time (shuttles, entrance fees, parking, routes, pets, etc):_____

NOTES / JOURNALING

HIKING LOGBOOK

DATE: ☼ ⛅ ☁ ☂ ⛈ ❄ 🌫 ☐Hot ☐Cold ☐Mild

Start Time:_____   End Time:_____

Total Duration:_____   Total Distance:_____

Elevation Gain/Loss:_____

Trail Type (circle one):   Out & Back   Loop   One Way / Shuttle

THE HIKE   ☆ ☆ ☆ ☆ ☆

City/State:_____

Trail(s):_____
_____

Start Latitude/Longitude:_____

Terrain:_____

Cell Phone Reception/Carrier:_____

☐First Visit   ☐Return Visit   Personal Rating: Easy / Intermediate / Difficult

Companion(s):_____

Facilities / Water Availability?:_____

Trail & Weather Conditions:_____

Observances (wildlife, nature, views, etc):_____

Gear, Food & Beverages:_____

Notes for next time (shuttles, entrance fees, parking, routes, pets, etc):_____
_____

NOTES / JOURNALING

HIKING LOGBOOK

DATE: ☼ ⛅ ☁ 🌧 ⛈ ❄ 🌫 ☐Hot ☐Cold ☐Mild

Start Time:_____   End Time:_____

Total Duration:_____   Total Distance:_____

Elevation Gain/Loss:_____

Trail Type (circle one):   Out & Back   Loop   One Way / Shuttle

THE HIKE   ☆ ☆ ☆ ☆ ☆

City/State:_____

Trail(s):_____

Start Latitude/Longitude:_____

Terrain:_____

Cell Phone Reception/Carrier:_____

☐First Visit   ☐Return Visit   Personal Rating: Easy / Intermediate / Difficult

Companion(s):_____

Facilities / Water Availability?:_____

Trail & Weather Conditions:_____

Observances (wildlife, nature, views, etc):_____

Gear, Food & Beverages:_____

Notes for next time (shuttles, entrance fees, parking, routes, pets, etc):_____

NOTES / JOURNALING

HIKING LOGBOOK

DATE: ☼ ⛅ ☁ ☁ 🌧 ⛈ ❄ 🌫 ☐Hot ☐Cold ☐Mild

Start Time:_____ End Time:_____

Total Duration:_____ Total Distance:_____

Elevation Gain/Loss:_____

Trail Type (circle one):   Out & Back   Loop   One Way / Shuttle

THE HIKE ☆☆☆☆☆

City/State:_____

Trail(s):_____
_____

Start Latitude/Longitude:_____

Terrain:_____

Cell Phone Reception/Carrier:_____

☐First Visit ☐Return Visit   Personal Rating: Easy / Intermediate / Difficult

Companion(s):_____

Facilities / Water Availability?:_____

Trail & Weather Conditions:_____

Observances (wildlife, nature, views, etc):_____

Gear, Food & Beverages:_____

Notes for next time (shuttles, entrance fees, parking, routes, pets, etc):_____
_____

NOTES / JOURNALING

HIKING LOGBOOK

DATE: ☀ ⛅ ☁ 🌧 ⛈ ❄ 🌫 ☐Hot ☐Cold ☐Mild

Start Time:_____ End Time:_____

Total Duration:_____ Total Distance:_____

Elevation Gain/Loss:_____

Trail Type (circle one):   Out & Back   Loop   One Way / Shuttle

THE HIKE   ☆ ☆ ☆ ☆ ☆

City/State:_____

Trail(s):_____
_____

Start Latitude/Longitude:_____

Terrain:_____

Cell Phone Reception/Carrier:_____

☐First Visit   ☐Return Visit   Personal Rating: Easy / Intermediate / Difficult

Companion(s):_____
_____

Facilities / Water Availability?:_____
_____

Trail & Weather Conditions:_____
_____

Observances (wildlife, nature, views, etc):_____
_____

Gear, Food & Beverages:_____
_____

Notes for next time (shuttles, entrance fees, parking, routes, pets, etc):_____
_____
_____

NOTES / JOURNALING

HIKING LOGBOOK

DATE: ☼ ⛅ ☁ ☂ ⛈ ❄ 🌫 ☐Hot ☐Cold ☐Mild

Start Time: _____ End Time: _____

Total Duration: _____ Total Distance: _____

Elevation Gain/Loss: _____

Trail Type (circle one):   Out & Back   Loop   One Way / Shuttle

THE HIKE   ☆ ☆ ☆ ☆ ☆

City/State: _____

Trail(s): _____

Start Latitude/Longitude: _____

Terrain: _____

Cell Phone Reception/Carrier: _____

☐First Visit   ☐Return Visit   Personal Rating: Easy / Intermediate / Difficult

Companion(s): _____

Facilities / Water Availability?: _____

Trail & Weather Conditions: _____

Observances (wildlife, nature, views, etc): _____

Gear, Food & Beverages: _____

Notes for next time (shuttles, entrance fees, parking, routes, pets, etc): _____

NOTES / JOURNALING

HIKING LOGBOOK

DATE: ☀ ⛅ ☁ ☁ ☂ ⚡ ❄ 🌫 ☐Hot ☐Cold ☐Mild

Start Time: _____ End Time: _____

Total Duration: _____ Total Distance: _____

Elevation Gain/Loss: _____

Trail Type (circle one):   Out & Back   Loop   One Way / Shuttle

THE HIKE ☆ ☆ ☆ ☆ ☆

City/State: _____

Trail(s): _____
_____

Start Latitude/Longitude: _____

Terrain: _____

Cell Phone Reception/Carrier: _____

☐First Visit   ☐Return Visit   Personal Rating: Easy / Intermediate / Difficult

Companion(s): _____
_____

Facilities / Water Availability?: _____
_____

Trail & Weather Conditions: _____
_____

Observances (wildlife, nature, views, etc): _____
_____

Gear, Food & Beverages: _____
_____

Notes for next time (shuttles, entrance fees, parking, routes, pets, etc):
_____
_____

NOTES / JOURNALING

HIKING LOGBOOK

DATE: ☀ ⛅ ☁ 🌧 ⛈ ❄ 🌫 ☐Hot ☐Cold ☐Mild

Start Time:_____ End Time:_____

Total Duration:_____ Total Distance:_____

Elevation Gain/Loss:_____

Trail Type (circle one):   Out & Back   Loop   One Way / Shuttle

THE HIKE ☆☆☆☆☆

City/State:_____

Trail(s):_____

Start Latitude/Longitude:_____

Terrain:_____

Cell Phone Reception/Carrier:_____

☐First Visit   ☐Return Visit   Personal Rating: Easy / Intermediate / Difficult

Companion(s):_____

Facilities / Water Availability?:_____

Trail & Weather Conditions:_____

Observances (wildlife, nature, views, etc):_____

Gear, Food & Beverages:_____

Notes for next time (shuttles, entrance fees, parking, routes, pets, etc):_____

NOTES / JOURNALING

HIKING LOGBOOK

DATE: ☀ ⛅ ☁ 🌧 ⛈ ❄ 🌬 ☐Hot ☐Cold ☐Mild

Start Time:_____ End Time:_____

Total Duration:_____ Total Distance:_____

Elevation Gain/Loss:_____

Trail Type (circle one):   Out & Back   Loop   One Way / Shuttle

THE HIKE   ☆ ☆ ☆ ☆ ☆

City/State:_____

Trail(s):_____

Start Latitude/Longitude:_____

Terrain:_____

Cell Phone Reception/Carrier:_____

☐First Visit   ☐Return Visit   Personal Rating: Easy / Intermediate / Difficult

Companion(s):_____

Facilities / Water Availability?:_____

Trail & Weather Conditions:_____

Observances (wildlife, nature, views, etc):_____

Gear, Food & Beverages:_____

Notes for next time (shuttles, entrance fees, parking, routes, pets, etc):_____

NOTES / JOURNALING

HIKING LOGBOOK

DATE: ☼ ⛅ ☁ ☁ 🌦 🌩 ❄ 🌫 ☐Hot ☐Cold ☐Mild

Start Time:_____ End Time:_____

Total Duration:_____ Total Distance:_____

Elevation Gain/Loss:_____

Trail Type (circle one):   Out & Back   Loop   One Way / Shuttle

THE HIKE   ☆ ☆ ☆ ☆ ☆

City/State:_____

Trail(s):_____
_____

Start Latitude/Longitude:_____

Terrain:_____

Cell Phone Reception/Carrier:_____

☐First Visit   ☐Return Visit   Personal Rating: Easy / Intermediate / Difficult

Companion(s):_____
_____

Facilities / Water Availability?:_____
_____

Trail & Weather Conditions:_____
_____

Observances (wildlife, nature, views, etc):_____
_____

Gear, Food & Beverages:_____
_____

Notes for next time (shuttles, entrance fees, parking, routes, pets, etc):
_____
_____

NOTES / JOURNALING

HIKING LOGBOOK

DATE: ☼ ⛅ ☁ 🌧 ⛈ ❄ 🌫 ☐Hot ☐Cold ☐Mild

Start Time: _____ End Time: _____

Total Duration: _____ Total Distance: _____

Elevation Gain/Loss: _____

Trail Type (circle one):   Out & Back   Loop   One Way / Shuttle

THE HIKE   ☆☆☆☆☆

City/State: _____

Trail(s): _____

Start Latitude/Longitude: _____

Terrain: _____

Cell Phone Reception/Carrier: _____

☐First Visit   ☐Return Visit   Personal Rating: Easy / Intermediate / Difficult

Companion(s): _____

Facilities / Water Availability?: _____

Trail & Weather Conditions: _____

Observances (wildlife, nature, views, etc): _____

Gear, Food & Beverages: _____

Notes for next time (shuttles, entrance fees, parking, routes, pets, etc): _____

NOTES / JOURNALING

HIKING LOGBOOK

DATE: ☀ ⛅ ☁ 🌧 ⛈ ❄ 🌫 ☐Hot ☐Cold ☐Mild

Start Time:_____ End Time:_____

Total Duration:_____ Total Distance:_____

Elevation Gain/Loss:_____

Trail Type (circle one):   Out & Back   Loop   One Way / Shuttle

THE HIKE ☆☆☆☆☆

City/State:_____

Trail(s):_____

Start Latitude/Longitude:_____

Terrain:_____

Cell Phone Reception/Carrier:_____

☐First Visit ☐Return Visit   Personal Rating: Easy / Intermediate / Difficult

Companion(s):_____

Facilities / Water Availability?:_____

Trail & Weather Conditions:_____

Observances (wildlife, nature, views, etc):_____

Gear, Food & Beverages:_____

Notes for next time (shuttles, entrance fees, parking, routes, pets, etc):_____

NOTES / JOURNALING

HIKING LOGBOOK

DATE: ☼ ⛅ ☁ ☁ 🌧 ❄ 🌬 ☐Hot ☐Cold ☐Mild

Start Time: _____ End Time: _____

Total Duration: _____ Total Distance: _____

Elevation Gain/Loss: _____

Trail Type (circle one):　Out & Back　　Loop　　One Way / Shuttle

THE HIKE　　☆ ☆ ☆ ☆ ☆

City/State: _____

Trail(s): _____
_____

Start Latitude/Longitude: _____

Terrain: _____

Cell Phone Reception/Carrier: _____

☐First Visit　☐Return Visit　　Personal Rating: Easy / Intermediate / Difficult

Companion(s): _____

Facilities / Water Availability?: _____

Trail & Weather Conditions: _____

Observances (wildlife, nature, views, etc): _____

Gear, Food & Beverages: _____

Notes for next time (shuttles, entrance fees, parking, routes, pets, etc): _____
_____

NOTES / JOURNALING

HIKING LOGBOOK

DATE: ☼ ⛅ ☁ 🌧 ⛈ ❄ 🌫 ☐Hot ☐Cold ☐Mild

Start Time: _____ End Time: _____

Total Duration: _____ Total Distance: _____

Elevation Gain/Loss: _____

Trail Type (circle one):   Out & Back   Loop   One Way / Shuttle

THE HIKE ☆☆☆☆☆

City/State: _____

Trail(s): _____

Start Latitude/Longitude: _____

Terrain: _____

Cell Phone Reception/Carrier: _____

☐First Visit   ☐Return Visit   Personal Rating: Easy / Intermediate / Difficult

Companion(s): _____

Facilities / Water Availability?: _____

Trail & Weather Conditions: _____

Observances (wildlife, nature, views, etc): _____

Gear, Food & Beverages: _____

Notes for next time (shuttles, entrance fees, parking, routes, pets, etc): _____

NOTES / JOURNALING

HIKING LOGBOOK

DATE: ☀ ⛅ ☁ 🌧 🌦 ❄ 🌫 ☐Hot ☐Cold ☐Mild

Start Time:_____   End Time:_____

Total Duration:_____   Total Distance:_____

Elevation Gain/Loss:_____

Trail Type (circle one):   Out & Back   Loop   One Way / Shuttle

THE HIKE ☆☆☆☆☆

City/State:_____

Trail(s):_____

Start Latitude/Longitude:_____

Terrain:_____

Cell Phone Reception/Carrier:_____

☐First Visit ☐Return Visit   Personal Rating: Easy / Intermediate / Difficult

Companion(s):_____

Facilities / Water Availability?:_____

Trail & Weather Conditions:_____

Observances (wildlife, nature, views, etc):_____

Gear, Food & Beverages:_____

Notes for next time (shuttles, entrance fees, parking, routes, pets, etc):_____

NOTES / JOURNALING

HIKING LOGBOOK

DATE: ☼ ⛅ ☁ ☁ 🌧 🌨 ❄ 🌬 ☐Hot ☐Cold ☐Mild

Start Time:_____ End Time:_____

Total Duration:_____ Total Distance:_____

Elevation Gain/Loss:_____

Trail Type (circle one):   Out & Back   Loop   One Way / Shuttle

THE HIKE ☆ ☆ ☆ ☆ ☆

City/State:_____

Trail(s):_____

Start Latitude/Longitude:_____

Terrain:_____

Cell Phone Reception/Carrier:_____

☐First Visit   ☐Return Visit   Personal Rating: Easy / Intermediate / Difficult

Companion(s):_____

Facilities / Water Availability?:_____

Trail & Weather Conditions:_____

Observances (wildlife, nature, views, etc):_____

Gear, Food & Beverages:_____

Notes for next time (shuttles, entrance fees, parking, routes, pets, etc):_____

NOTES / JOURNALING

HIKING LOGBOOK

DATE: ☀ ⛅ ☁ 🌥 ⛈ ❄ 🌫 ☐Hot ☐Cold ☐Mild

Start Time:_____ End Time:_____

Total Duration:_____ Total Distance:_____

Elevation Gain/Loss:_____

Trail Type (circle one): Out & Back Loop One Way / Shuttle

THE HIKE ☆☆☆☆☆

City/State:_____

Trail(s):_____

Start Latitude/Longitude:_____

Terrain:_____

Cell Phone Reception/Carrier:_____

☐First Visit ☐Return Visit Personal Rating: Easy / Intermediate / Difficult

Companion(s):_____

Facilities / Water Availability?:_____

Trail & Weather Conditions:_____

Observances (wildlife, nature, views, etc):_____

Gear, Food & Beverages:_____

Notes for next time (shuttles, entrance fees, parking, routes, pets, etc):_____

NOTES / JOURNALING

HIKING LOGBOOK

DATE: ☀ ⛅ ☁ 🌧 ⛈ ❄ 🌫 ☐Hot ☐Cold ☐Mild

Start Time:_____ End Time:_____

Total Duration:_____ Total Distance:_____

Elevation Gain/Loss:_____

Trail Type (circle one):   Out & Back   Loop   One Way / Shuttle

THE HIKE   ☆☆☆☆☆

City/State:_____

Trail(s):_____

Start Latitude/Longitude:_____

Terrain:_____

Cell Phone Reception/Carrier:_____

☐First Visit ☐Return Visit   Personal Rating: Easy / Intermediate / Difficult

Companion(s):_____

Facilities / Water Availability?:_____

Trail & Weather Conditions:_____

Observances (wildlife, nature, views, etc):_____

Gear, Food & Beverages:_____

Notes for next time (shuttles, entrance fees, parking, routes, pets, etc):_____

NOTES / JOURNALING

HIKING LOGBOOK

DATE: ☀ ⛅ ☁ 🌧 ⛈ ❄ 🌫 □Hot □Cold □Mild

Start Time: _____   End Time: _____

Total Duration: _____   Total Distance: _____

Elevation Gain/Loss: _____

Trail Type (circle one):   Out & Back   Loop   One Way / Shuttle

THE HIKE   ☆ ☆ ☆ ☆ ☆

City/State: _____

Trail(s): _____
_____

Start Latitude/Longitude: _____

Terrain: _____

Cell Phone Reception/Carrier: _____

□First Visit   □Return Visit   Personal Rating: Easy / Intermediate / Difficult

Companion(s): _____
_____

Facilities / Water Availability?: _____
_____

Trail & Weather Conditions: _____
_____

Observances (wildlife, nature, views, etc): _____
_____

Gear, Food & Beverages: _____
_____

Notes for next time (shuttles, entrance fees, parking, routes, pets, etc): _____
_____

NOTES / JOURNALING

HIKING LOGBOOK

DATE: ☀ ⛅ ☁ ☂ ⛈ ❄ 🌫 ☐Hot ☐Cold ☐Mild

Start Time:_____ End Time:_____

Total Duration:_____ Total Distance:_____

Elevation Gain/Loss:_____

Trail Type (circle one):   Out & Back   Loop   One Way / Shuttle

THE HIKE   ☆ ☆ ☆ ☆ ☆

City/State:_____

Trail(s):_____

Start Latitude/Longitude:_____

Terrain:_____

Cell Phone Reception/Carrier:_____

☐First Visit   ☐Return Visit   Personal Rating: Easy / Intermediate / Difficult

Companion(s):_____

Facilities / Water Availability?:_____

Trail & Weather Conditions:_____

Observances (wildlife, nature, views, etc):_____

Gear, Food & Beverages:_____

Notes for next time (shuttles, entrance fees, parking, routes, pets, etc):_____

NOTES / JOURNALING

HIKING LOGBOOK

DATE: ☀ ⛅ ☁ 🌧 🌦 ❄ 🌬 ☐Hot ☐Cold ☐Mild

Start Time: _____ End Time: _____

Total Duration: _____ Total Distance: _____

Elevation Gain/Loss: _____

Trail Type (circle one):   Out & Back   Loop   One Way / Shuttle

THE HIKE ☆☆☆☆☆

City/State: _____

Trail(s): _____
_____

Start Latitude/Longitude: _____

Terrain: _____

Cell Phone Reception/Carrier: _____

☐First Visit   ☐Return Visit   Personal Rating: Easy / Intermediate / Difficult

Companion(s): _____
_____

Facilities / Water Availability?: _____
_____

Trail & Weather Conditions: _____
_____

Observances (wildlife, nature, views, etc): _____
_____

Gear, Food & Beverages: _____
_____

Notes for next time (shuttles, entrance fees, parking, routes, pets, etc): ___
_____
_____

NOTES / JOURNALING

HIKING LOGBOOK

DATE: ☼ ⛅ ☁ ☂ ⚡ ❄ 🌫 ☐Hot ☐Cold ☐Mild

Start Time: _____ End Time: _____

Total Duration: _____ Total Distance: _____

Elevation Gain/Loss: _____

Trail Type (circle one):   Out & Back   Loop   One Way / Shuttle

THE HIKE ☆☆☆☆☆

City/State: _____

Trail(s): _____

Start Latitude/Longitude: _____

Terrain: _____

Cell Phone Reception/Carrier: _____

☐First Visit   ☐Return Visit   Personal Rating: Easy / Intermediate / Difficult

Companion(s): _____

Facilities / Water Availability?: _____

Trail & Weather Conditions: _____

Observances (wildlife, nature, views, etc): _____

Gear, Food & Beverages: _____

Notes for next time (shuttles, entrance fees, parking, routes, pets, etc): _____

NOTES / JOURNALING

HIKING LOGBOOK

DATE: ☼ ⛅ ☁ ☁ ⛈ ❄ 🌫 □Hot □Cold □Mild

Start Time: _____ End Time: _____

Total Duration: _____ Total Distance: _____

Elevation Gain/Loss: _____

Trail Type (circle one):   Out & Back   Loop   One Way / Shuttle

THE HIKE ☆ ☆ ☆ ☆ ☆

City/State: _____

Trail(s): _____

Start Latitude/Longitude: _____

Terrain: _____

Cell Phone Reception/Carrier: _____

□First Visit   □Return Visit   Personal Rating: Easy / Intermediate / Difficult

Companion(s): _____

Facilities / Water Availability?: _____

Trail & Weather Conditions: _____

Observances (wildlife, nature, views, etc): _____

Gear, Food & Beverages: _____

Notes for next time (shuttles, entrance fees, parking, routes, pets, etc): _____

NOTES / JOURNALING

HIKING LOGBOOK

DATE: ☀ ⛅ ☁ 🌧 ⛈ ❄ 🌫 ☐Hot ☐Cold ☐Mild

Start Time: _____ End Time: _____

Total Duration: _____ Total Distance: _____

Elevation Gain/Loss: _____

Trail Type (circle one):　　Out & Back　　Loop　　One Way / Shuttle

THE HIKE　　　　　　　　　　☆☆☆☆☆

City/State: _____

Trail(s): _____

_____

Start Latitude/Longitude: _____

Terrain: _____

Cell Phone Reception/Carrier: _____

☐First Visit　☐Return Visit　　Personal Rating: Easy / Intermediate / Difficult

Companion(s): _____

_____

Facilities / Water Availability?: _____

_____

Trail & Weather Conditions: _____

_____

Observances (wildlife, nature, views, etc): _____

_____

Gear, Food & Beverages: _____

_____

Notes for next time (shuttles, entrance fees, parking, routes, pets, etc): _____

_____

_____

NOTES / JOURNALING

HIKING LOGBOOK

DATE: ☀ ⛅ ☁ ☁ ☔ 🌦 ❄ 🌫 ☐Hot ☐Cold ☐Mild

Start Time:_____ End Time:_____

Total Duration:_____ Total Distance:_____

Elevation Gain/Loss:_____

Trail Type (circle one):   Out & Back   Loop   One Way / Shuttle

THE HIKE ☆ ☆ ☆ ☆ ☆

City/State:_____

Trail(s):_____

Start Latitude/Longitude:_____

Terrain:_____

Cell Phone Reception/Carrier:_____

☐First Visit   ☐Return Visit   Personal Rating: Easy / Intermediate / Difficult

Companion(s):_____

Facilities / Water Availability?:_____

Trail & Weather Conditions:_____

Observances (wildlife, nature, views, etc):_____

Gear, Food & Beverages:_____

Notes for next time (shuttles, entrance fees, parking, routes, pets, etc):_____

NOTES / JOURNALING

HIKING LOGBOOK

DATE: ☼ ⛅ ☁ ☂ ⛈ ❄ ☁ ☐Hot ☐Cold ☐Mild

Start Time: _____ End Time: _____

Total Duration: _____ Total Distance: _____

Elevation Gain/Loss: _____

Trail Type (circle one):   Out & Back   Loop   One Way / Shuttle

THE HIKE   ☆ ☆ ☆ ☆ ☆

City/State: _____

Trail(s): _____

Start Latitude/Longitude: _____

Terrain: _____

Cell Phone Reception/Carrier: _____

☐First Visit   ☐Return Visit   Personal Rating: Easy / Intermediate / Difficult

Companion(s): _____

Facilities / Water Availability?: _____

Trail & Weather Conditions: _____

Observances (wildlife, nature, views, etc): _____

Gear, Food & Beverages: _____

Notes for next time (shuttles, entrance fees, parking, routes, pets, etc): _____

NOTES / JOURNALING

HIKING LOGBOOK

DATE: ☼ ⛅ ☁ ☂ ⛈ ❄ 🌫 ☐Hot ☐Cold ☐Mild

Start Time:_____ End Time:_____

Total Duration:_____ Total Distance:_____

Elevation Gain/Loss:_____

Trail Type (circle one):   Out & Back   Loop   One Way / Shuttle

THE HIKE ☆☆☆☆☆

City/State:_____

Trail(s):_____

Start Latitude/Longitude:_____

Terrain:_____

Cell Phone Reception/Carrier:_____

☐First Visit ☐Return Visit   Personal Rating: Easy / Intermediate / Difficult

Companion(s):_____

Facilities / Water Availability?:_____

Trail & Weather Conditions:_____

Observances (wildlife, nature, views, etc):_____

Gear, Food & Beverages:_____

Notes for next time (shuttles, entrance fees, parking, routes, pets, etc):_____

NOTES / JOURNALING

HIKING LOGBOOK

DATE: ☼ ⛅ ☁ ☁ 🌧 ⛈ ❄ 🌫 ☐Hot ☐Cold ☐Mild

Start Time:_____ End Time:_____

Total Duration:_____ Total Distance:_____

Elevation Gain/Loss: _____

Trail Type (circle one): Out & Back Loop One Way / Shuttle

THE HIKE ☆ ☆ ☆ ☆ ☆

City/State:_____

Trail(s):_____

Start Latitude/Longitude:_____

Terrain:_____

Cell Phone Reception/Carrier:_____

☐First Visit ☐Return Visit Personal Rating: Easy / Intermediate / Difficult

Companion(s):_____

Facilities / Water Availability?:_____

Trail & Weather Conditions:_____

Observances (wildlife, nature, views, etc):_____

Gear, Food & Beverages:_____

Notes for next time (shuttles, entrance fees, parking, routes, pets, etc):_____

NOTES / JOURNALING

HIKING LOGBOOK

DATE: ☀ ⛅ ☁ 🌧 ⛈ ❄ 🌫 ☐Hot ☐Cold ☐Mild

Start Time: _____ End Time: _____

Total Duration: _____ Total Distance: _____

Elevation Gain/Loss: _____

Trail Type (circle one):   Out & Back   Loop   One Way / Shuttle

THE HIKE ☆☆☆☆☆

City/State: _____

Trail(s): _____

Start Latitude/Longitude: _____

Terrain: _____

Cell Phone Reception/Carrier: _____

☐First Visit   ☐Return Visit   Personal Rating: Easy / Intermediate / Difficult

Companion(s): _____

Facilities / Water Availability?: _____

Trail & Weather Conditions: _____

Observances (wildlife, nature, views, etc): _____

Gear, Food & Beverages: _____

Notes for next time (shuttles, entrance fees, parking, routes, pets, etc): _____

NOTES / JOURNALING

HIKING LOGBOOK

DATE: ☀ ⛅ ☁ 🌧 ⛈ ❄ 🌫 ☐Hot ☐Cold ☐Mild

Start Time:_____   End Time:_____

Total Duration:_____   Total Distance:_____

Elevation Gain/Loss:_____

Trail Type (circle one):   Out & Back   Loop   One Way / Shuttle

THE HIKE   ☆☆☆☆☆

City/State:_____

Trail(s):_____
_____

Start Latitude/Longitude:_____

Terrain:_____

Cell Phone Reception/Carrier:_____

☐First Visit   ☐Return Visit   Personal Rating: Easy / Intermediate / Difficult

Companion(s):_____
_____

Facilities / Water Availability?:_____
_____

Trail & Weather Conditions:_____
_____

Observances (wildlife, nature, views, etc):_____
_____

Gear, Food & Beverages:_____
_____

Notes for next time (shuttles, entrance fees, parking, routes, pets, etc):_____
_____
_____

NOTES / JOURNALING

HIKING LOGBOOK

DATE: ☼ ⛅ ☁ ☁ ☂ ⛈ ❄ 🌫 ☐Hot ☐Cold ☐Mild

Start Time:_____ **End Time:**_____

Total Duration: _____ **Total Distance:** _____

Elevation Gain/Loss: _____

Trail Type (circle one):   Out & Back   Loop   One Way / Shuttle

THE HIKE   ☆ ☆ ☆ ☆ ☆

City/State:_____

Trail(s):_____

_____

Start Latitude/Longitude:_____

Terrain:_____

Cell Phone Reception/Carrier:_____

☐First Visit   ☐Return Visit   **Personal Rating:** Easy / Intermediate / Difficult

Companion(s):_____

Facilities / Water Availability?:_____

Trail & Weather Conditions:_____

Observances (wildlife, nature, views, etc):_____

Gear, Food & Beverages:_____

Notes for next time (shuttles, entrance fees, parking, routes, pets, etc):_____

NOTES / JOURNALING

HIKING LOGBOOK

DATE: ☼ ⛅ ☁ ☂ ⛈ ❄ 🌫 □Hot □Cold □Mild

Start Time: _____ End Time: _____

Total Duration: _____ Total Distance: _____

Elevation Gain/Loss: _____

Trail Type (circle one): Out & Back   Loop   One Way / Shuttle

THE HIKE ☆ ☆ ☆ ☆ ☆

City/State: _____

Trail(s): _____

Start Latitude/Longitude: _____

Terrain: _____

Cell Phone Reception/Carrier: _____

□First Visit □Return Visit   Personal Rating: Easy / Intermediate / Difficult

Companion(s): _____

Facilities / Water Availability?: _____

Trail & Weather Conditions: _____

Observances (wildlife, nature, views, etc): _____

Gear, Food & Beverages: _____

Notes for next time (shuttles, entrance fees, parking, routes, pets, etc): _____

NOTES / JOURNALING

Made in the USA
Monee, IL
15 December 2020